Oct 2014

Kansas City, MO Public Library

D1212908

Earth's GROSSEST Animals

Weird Animals in the Wild

Alix Wood

WINDMILL BOOKS

New York

Published in 2014 by Windmill Books, An Imprint of Rosen Publishing
29 East 21st Street, New York, NY 10010

Copyright © 2014 Alix Wood Books

All rights reserved. No part of this book may be reproduced in any form
without permission in writing from the publisher, except by a reviewer.

Editor: Sara Howell
Designer: Alix Wood
Consultant: Sally Morgan

Photo Credits: Cover, 27 top and bottom, 29 bottom © Fotolia; 1, 4, 5, 6, 7 bottom, 8, 9, 10, 11,
12, 13, 14, 15, 16, 17, 18, 19, 20, 21 top, 22, 23 top, 24 top, 25, 28, 29 top © Shutterstock; 7 top
© Cliff1066; 21 bottom © Cyril Ruoso/Minden Pictures/FLPA; 23 bottom © Gustavocarra ; 24
bottom © Gary Nafis; 26 © Pete Oxford/Minden Pictures/FLPA;

Library of Congress Cataloging-in-Publication Data

Wood, Alix.
Weird animals in the wild / by Alix Wood.
    pages cm. — (Earth's grossest animals)
Includes index.
ISBN 978-1-61533-735-4 (library binding) — ISBN 978-1-61533-787-3 (pbk.) —
ISBN 978-1-61533-788-0 (6-pack)
1. Animals—Juvenile literature. I. Title.
QL49.W6945 2014
590—dc23
                                    2012048295

Manufactured in the United States of America

CPSIA Compliance Information: Batch #BS13WM: For Further Information contact Windmill Books, New York, New York at 1-866-478-0556

Contents

What's Gross in the Wild?

Some animals are gross because they are plain ugly. Some animals have really bad manners, and some are deadly.

A warthog will never win any beauty prizes. It has a lumpy head and big tusks. Its tusks are used for digging, fighting other hogs, and for defense against **predators**. The shorter lower tusks get razor sharp from rubbing against the upper pair when the warthog's mouth opens and closes.

A warthog looks fierce, but it often runs away from a fight or hides in a burrow. It can run as fast as 34 miles per hour (55 km/h)!

A warthog holds its tail up like a warning flag when it runs.

A slow loris (left) looks cute, but it can be pretty gross, too! It makes a lethal mixture of saliva and liquid from a **gland** in its elbow. The female covers her young with the liquid while she leaves to search for food. The smell deters most predators! If a predator bites a loris, the mixture can poison them.

a male lion guarding the kill

Even though it is the female lions that do the hunting, the male lions always eat first. After they eat, the females get their turn. When the females are finished, the cubs are allowed to eat. Lions don't have very good table manners!

Freaky Creatures

Some wild animals just look bizarre. This selection have to be some of the weirdest looking creatures to walk this Earth.

This strange-looking giant anteater can grow to 7 feet (2.1 m) long! An anteater has no teeth. It uses its long tongue to lap up the thousands of ants and termites it eats each day. It can flick its tongue up to 160 times per minute. The anteater uses its sharp claws to tear open anthills.

An anteater can rear up on its back legs and lash out with its 4-inch-(10 cm) long claws.

a pink fairy armadillo

Pink fairy armadillos have a cute name, but they don't look that cute. They are pink, about the size of a rat, and armed with huge claws on their forelegs. They can bury themselves under the sand in seconds. They also "sand-swim," or paddle through the sand as though they were swimming through water.

The platypus (right) looks so weird people used to think it was a **hoax**! It is one of the few **mammals** that lays eggs. It also has some pretty unusual ways to defend itself. The male platypus has sharp, poisonous spurs on its rear legs. When attacked the platypus kicks and injects venom with its spurs.

A platypus' snout is actually quite soft and covered with receptors which help the platypus find its **prey**.

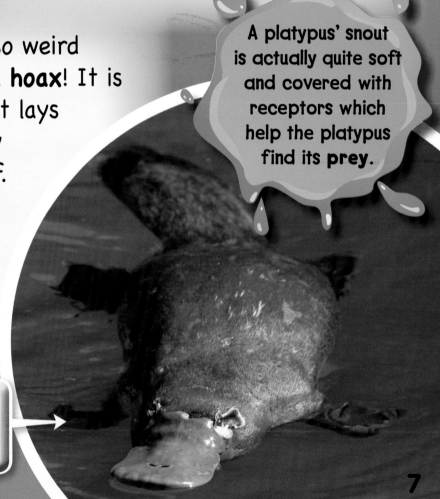

A platypus has a tail like a beaver, a body like an otter, has **webbed** feet, a beak like a bird, and it lays eggs!

Ugly Monkeys

Monkeys are like humans in many ways. Not many people would want to look like these two, though!

Neither end of a baboon is that pretty. Baboons can be fierce, too. They eat fruits and roots, but also like to eat meat. They will hunt birds, **rodents**, and young, large mammals, such as baby antelope.

Male baboons scare off predators like leopards or cheetahs by forming a line and strutting in a threatening way. They bare their large, canine teeth and scream.

sharp canine teeth

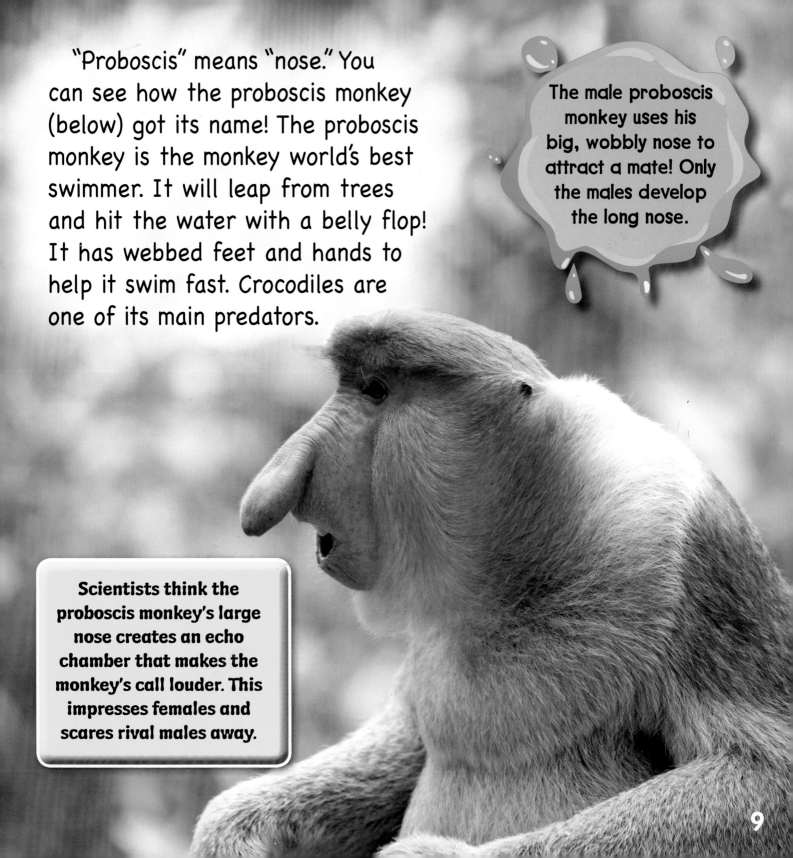

"Proboscis" means "nose." You can see how the proboscis monkey (below) got its name! The proboscis monkey is the monkey world's best swimmer. It will leap from trees and hit the water with a belly flop! It has webbed feet and hands to help it swim fast. Crocodiles are one of its main predators.

The male proboscis monkey uses his big, wobbly nose to attract a mate! Only the males develop the long nose.

Scientists think the proboscis monkey's large nose creates an echo chamber that makes the monkey's call louder. This impresses females and scares rival males away.

Dung Makers and Friends

Elephants are the largest land-living mammals in the world. They have amazing trunks that can do all kinds of things.

This African elephant (right) used to be light gray! Elephants love to roll around in the mud. The mud acts as sunscreen and keeps the elephant cool. It also acts as a barrier to keep off insects.

An elephant uses its trunk to suck up wet mud and spray it over its body.

When eating and drinking, an elephant's trunk and mouth are both used for different things. The trunk selects and prepares the mouthful, and then passes it to the mouth for chewing and swallowing.

trunk

An adult elephant produces 9 pounds (20 kg) of **dung** a day! The dung is a great source of food for this vervet monkey (right). It doesn't eat it, though. The monkey is searching the dung to find insects to eat!

An elephant can use its trunk as a weapon, to gather food, to suck up water to drink, and to spray water to give itself a shower.

The elephant's trunk is able to sense the size, shape, and temperature of an object. The tip of the trunk ends in a sort of finger which is so sensitive it can pick up a small pin. An elephant uses its tusks for digging and finding food. An elephant can even use its tusks to dig for water underground.

This elephant is using its trunk to breathe like a snorkel as it swims.

Hippo Habits

Hippopotamuses kill more people each year than any other animal, including lions and tigers. Hippos are actually plant eaters, though. They only attack people if the people are between them and deep water, or between them and their young.

An adult hippo weighs around 3 tons (2,700 kg) and can run three times faster than a person. If a hippo is threatened on land, it'll run for water, and you don't want to be in the way!

A hippo can open its mouth almost 150 degrees. Its huge teeth sharpen themselves as they grind together. A hippo's large canine teeth can grow as long as 20 inches (50 cm)!

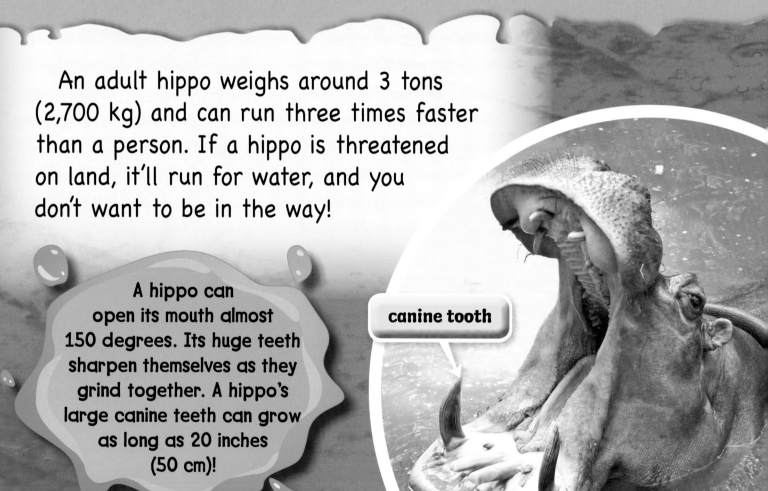

canine tooth

If they breathe out, hippos can make themselves sink so they can run along the floor of lakes and rivers. They need to find a slope to get back out again.

a hippo running underwater

Hippos secrete an oily, red liquid to protect their skin from the Sun. People used to think hippos were sweating blood.

To attract a female, a male hippo has a disgusting habit. While he is going to the bathroom, he will spin his tail like a rotor, flinging the mixture of **urine** and dung far and wide. Apparently the females love this!

hippos greeting each other with a dung-flinging display

13

Amazing Tongues

Several animals have amazingly long and useful tongues. A giraffe's tongue is around 18 inches (45 cm) long and very slobbery!

A giraffe (left) uses its long tongue to reach high leaves. The giraffe's slimy drool coats prickly leaves and makes them easier to swallow. Giraffes like to wipe their slobbery faces on other giraffes!

Male giraffes taste the female's urine with their tongues to see if she is ready to mate!

A giraffe uses its long tongue to clean out its nostrils!

Cattle like to clean out their nose with their tongue, and that's not their only revolting habit. Cows burp almost constantly to relieve gas from their stomachs. They can produce 74 gallons (280 l) of gas a day from their front and back ends combined!

Big cats use their rough tongues to clean themselves and each other. Their tongues have hooked, backward-facing spines that work like a hairbrush to detangle fur.

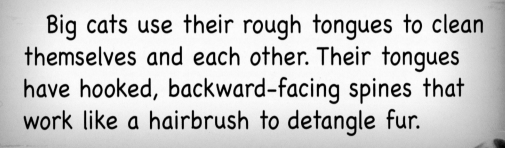

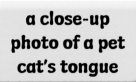

a close-up photo of a pet cat's tongue

Monsters and Dragons

The **Gila monster** and the **Komodo dragon** are both huge, fearsome lizards. One has deadly saliva and the other hunts deer!

A Gila monster only eats between five and ten times a year, but its meals are usually about a third of its body size! Prey is either crushed to death, swallowed whole, or bitten with its **venomous** jaws! The Gila monster loves to eat eggs and can track them with its great sense of smell. It can climb trees to find eggs, or dig them up with its powerful claws.

Gila monsters have been seen flipping over while biting their victims, probably to help the flow of the venom into the wound.

Komodo dragons often hunt their prey in groups, which is very unusual for a reptile. They mainly eat deer, insects, birds, and mammals. They also **scavenge** food that other animals have killed. Komodo dragons occasionally attack humans. They have about 60 jagged teeth which they replace if they lose any. Their saliva contains deadly **bacteria** which stops their victim's blood from clotting. Even if their prey runs off, the dragons will slowly follow it, as the victim will usually die from its wounds.

A Komodo dragon's saliva is often stained with blood, because its teeth are almost completely hidden by its gums. The teeth break through the gums during feeding!

a Komodo dragon eating a goat

Anger Management

Llamas and camels are close relatives in the animal kingdom. One thing they have in common are their bad manners!

Llamas are very social herd animals, but sometimes they spit at each other as a way of keeping lower-ranked llamas in their place!

You can tell how annoyed a llama is by its spit! The more irritated the llama is, the further back into its three stomachs it goes to draw materials for its spit. Llamas fight each other by spitting, ramming each other with their chests, neck wrestling, and kicking, mainly to knock the other off balance.

Camels are well-known for being stubborn. They sometimes vomit on each other when they are angry! Camels can go for days without eating and drinking. They live off the stored fat in the humps on their backs. When camels do drink they drink a lot! A very thirsty animal can drink 30 gallons (135 l) of water in around 13 minutes!

A camel can close its nostrils between breaths to keep the sand out.

This camel is looking for a mate. He froths at the mouth and pushes an inflatable organ in his neck called a "dulla" out of his mouth. He will also throw urine over his back with his tail. How attractive!

Turtles and Tortoises

A tortoise is a land turtle with a high domed shell. Turtles have flatter shells as the shape helps them swim through water.

A tortoise defends itself by emptying its bladder if it is picked up. A desert tortoise stores water in its bladder, and can survive for a year or more without food or water! Emptying its bladder could mean the desert tortoise dehydrates if it can't find water quickly.

The pancake tortoise (below) has a flat shell. It wedges itself between narrow rocks if threatened and **inflates** itself with air! This makes it nearly impossible to pull out from the rocks.

A tortoise has a horny beak and no teeth.

The alligator snapping turtle has a red wormlike **lure** in its mouth. When a curious fish gets close, the turtle's mouth snaps shut!

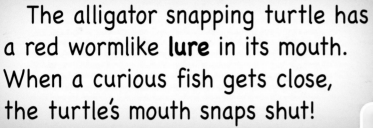

lure

The mata mata turtle (below) hides itself in the water by looking like bark and fallen leaves. When a fish swims near it opens its large mouth wide, creating a **vacuum** that sucks the prey into its mouth, which then snaps shut.

Some turtles breathe through their rear! Turtles have a vent called a "cloaca" which they use to lay eggs and get rid of waste. Some turtles also use this vent to take in **oxygen** from the water.

Weird Frogs

There are some gross frogs living in the wild. You can see a glass frog's heart pumping through its see-through body!

A Budgett's frog (below) has short legs and an enormous mouth. When it opens its mouth wide it can give a shrill scream made up of popping and whirring noises! A Budgett's frog has no teeth, but has two sharp lumps inside its mouth which it uses to chew. It has been known to bite people.

The glass frog's see-through body lets you see all its insides working away! Nice.

a Budgett's frog

A Budgett's frog looks like a flat pebble with eyes!

The tiny poison dart frog has enough poison to kill 20,000 mice! The insects the frog eats feed on plants that have **toxins**, which then pass to the frog. It catches its prey with a long, sticky tongue that darts out and hits them. It got its name because people used the frog's deadly poison on the tips of darts to hunt for food.

a poison dart frog

If it wasn't gross enough to be a frog with hair, the hairy frog produces claws by breaking bones in its toes and pushing them through its skin!

The hairy frog's hair is actually very thin bits of flesh that grow on the male's thighs and body. A hairy frog has very small lungs, so scientists believe the frills help it draw in extra oxygen by giving the frog more skin area.

Scary Snakes

Snakes have plenty of gross habits. They swallow their food whole, and they have flexible jaws so they can eat prey bigger than their head! They can kill people, too.

The black mamba (right) is large, fast, and deadly. Its poison attacks quickly. Twenty minutes after being bitten a victim is unable to talk. After six hours, without an **antidote**, the victim is dead.

a black mamba smelling the air with its tongue

When threatened, many snakes make a warning sound like a hiss or a rattle. This Arizona coral snake makes a loud farting noise! It may do this to draw attention away from its head.

A python squeezes the life out of its prey by coiling itself around it. With each breath the prey takes the snake will squeeze a little tighter until the prey animal stops breathing completely. The prey is then swallowed whole. If it eats a big meal, a python may only need to eat four to five times a year!

a green tree python

The spitting cobra spits its venom. If the venom goes in a victim's eyes it can blind them. The spitting cobra can spit venom 5-8 feet (2-3 m) and is a great shot. It does not often actually bite.

Tree Dwellers

In some places, if you look up, you will find the grossest creatures hanging around in trees!

The aye-aye has rodent-like teeth and a spooky, long, skinny middle finger. It has a weird way of finding food. The aye-aye taps on trees to find grubs, and then gnaws a small hole in the wood. It pokes its long, thin finger in the hole to pull the grubs out!

To find grubs, an aye-aye taps on a tree trunk up to eight times per second. It is listening for hollow areas which would echo. A hollow chamber means a grub may be inside.

Tarsiers are small animals with enormous eyes. Each eyeball is as large as its entire brain. They can turn their heads through 180 degrees in each direction, which is lucky because their eyes are so big they can't move in their heads! Tarsiers catch insects by jumping at them.

Tarsier's eyes are so big they would be the same as grapefruit-sized eyes in a human!

Sloths spend so long hanging from trees their fur grows upside down!

Sloths spend most of their life hanging in the trees. They are so slow tree moss grows on them! They have a powerful grip aided by their long claws. Dead sloths have been known to stay hanging from branches for some time!

Feeding Time

Animals' table manners are quite revolting. What they eat and the way they eat it can be pretty stomach churning. Vomit seems to be one of their favorite meals!

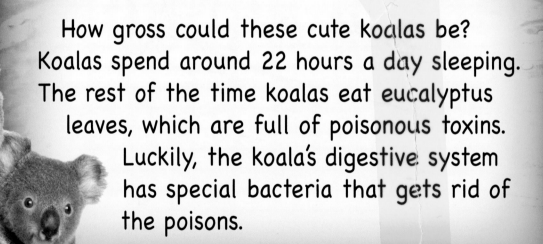

How gross could these cute koalas be? Koalas spend around 22 hours a day sleeping. The rest of the time koalas eat eucalyptus leaves, which are full of poisonous toxins. Luckily, the koala's digestive system has special bacteria that gets rid of the poisons.

Koalas smell like cough drops because of their diet of eucalyptus leaves!

Koala babies are not born with this bacteria. They have to build up their defenses by eating food that their mother has spit up!

Some animals, like this deer, store some of the food they eat in a special pouch in their stomach. They later cough up this food and begin to chew it again! The stored food is called "cud."

In the United States, about 200 people die each year when their car hits a deer in the road.

Jackals aren't fussy eaters. They'll eat rotting flesh, even if it has been rotting for days! Jackal pups also eat their parent's vomited food. Parents will eat their pups' vomit, too.

a mother jackal coughing up her food

Glossary

antidote (AN-tee-doht)
A remedy to counteract the effects of poison.

bacteria (bak-TIR-ee-uh)
Microorganisms that have chemical effects and disease-causing abilities.

dung (DUNG)
Waste matter of an animal.

gland (GLAND)
An organ that makes and secretes saliva, sweat, or bile from a plant or animal.

hoax (HOHKS)
Something false that people pretend is true.

inflates (in-FLAYTS)
Swell or fill with air or gas.

lure (LOOR)
A decoy for attracting animals to capture.

mammals (MA-mulz)
Animals that feed their young with milk, have a backbone, and have skin covered with hair.

oxygen (OK-sih-jen)
A tasteless, odorless gas that is necessary for life.

predators (PREH-duh-terz)
Animals that live by killing and eating other animals.

prey (PRAY)
An animal hunted or killed
by another animal for food.

rodents (ROH-dents)
Small mammals, for example
mice, squirrels, or beavers,
that have sharp front
teeth used for gnawing.

scavenge (SKA-venj)
To feed on dead or
decaying matter.

toxins (TOK-sunz)
Poisonous substances
produced by a
living organism.

urine (YUR-un)
Animal waste that is
usually a yellowish liquid in
mammals but semisolid in
birds and reptiles.

vacuum (VA-kyoom)
A space from which most of
the air has been removed.

venomous (VEH-nuh-mis)
Having or producing poison.

webbed (WEBD)
Flaps of thin skin between
toes and fingers.

WEBSITES
For web resources related to the
subject of this book, go to:
www.windmillbooks.com/weblinks
and select this book's title.

Read More

Antill, Sara. *An Elephant's Life*. Living Large. New York: PowerKids Press, 2012.

Guidone, Julie. *Sloths*. Animals That Live in the Rain Forest. New York: Weekly Reader Early Learning Library, 2009.

Kras, Sara Louise. *Koalas*. Australian Animals. Mankato, MN: Pebble Plus, 2010.

Index